The STUDENT'S DRINKING HANDBOOK

Containing everything a student should know about drinking and university life

Joe Varley

Fisher King Publishing

THE STUDENT'S DRINKING HANDBOOK

Copyright © JOE VARLEY 2021

PRINT ISBN 978-1-914560-09-5
Ebook ISBN 978-1-914560-26-2

Fisher King Publishing
The Old Barn
York Road
Thirsk
YO7 3AD
England
fisherkingpublishing.co.uk

"They speak of my drinking, but never question my thirst."

Proverb

Disclaimer: *This book intends to educate, advise, and to humour. The intention is not to glamorise the use of alcohol.*

Contents

About the author

Joe is a Yorkshire writer and attended a university in Wales (guess which one!). After graduating in zoology, he worked and drank his way around New Zealand, resulting in his novel *Hard Up Down Under*.

His favourite drink is cold lager, though he's partial to gin and tonic, whiskey (and Scotch), vodka, cider, rum, red and white wine, brandy, Champagne, shots and ale. And Guinness. If you see him around, please buy him a drink - he might even buy you one back.

View his Amazon Author Page for more information and books.

Introduction

You're thinking about university.

Why? Because you're 18 years old, give or take (lucky you!). You're also excited and nervous in equal measures. Not because of the recent A-Levels; you crammed in that last hour's revision before the tricky psychology exam, so you're confident enough. No, now you're waiting for the results that'll determine whether you'll make it to university. Excited and nervous? You bet you are.

Soon you'll know which university or college might have the pleasure of your company. It could even be your preferred choice. If you've done well, you won't be a pupil anymore. You'll be upgraded to a "student": one who studies. And, most likely, one who drinks.

The school routine will be a distant dream. You'll be buying train tickets or cadging a lift from your parents, safe in the knowledge that for the next three months (for the first semester at least) you'll be sleeping on hardboard masquerading as a mattress, and cooking for yourself (how long will eight tins of baked beans and a loaf of Warburtons last?). You'll also venture to at least one of numerous student bars and local hostelries…then repeat that for the next couple of years. Sounds idyllic, right?

Perhaps you're already a student. You'll probably have a "local" and know the best pubs for 2-4-1 booze offers. You think of Dave, the barman at The White Rose, as a legend, and the thought of a drink at 11.15am seems feasible. If that's the case, the transition from pupil to fully-fledged student is proving successful, so this handbook will serve as a "top up" to what you already know.

This book is written as a concise guide to supplement a student's lifestyle, like a lime wedge in a double G&T. Whilst a lot of students in the 18-21 age bracket will find it beneficial, mature students should also welcome the advice - they may even feel younger, if only temporarily.

With the turmoil of recent times, students should be itching to launch themselves into a life of studying, revising, rekindling new friendships and boozing. Things like COVID have affected almost everyone, and students have suffered both educationally, mentally and socially. But fear not! Your day will come once more.

When you're ready, keep the beers on ice, and read on. The drinking lecture starts now.

Chapter 1: Are you experienced?

So, you're a student now, eh? Good on you! Now adulthood starts. But not before a word to the wise. Think of this as an informative disclaimer, not as a horror story. Things will get more light-hearted.

Ethanol (that's alcohol to non-chemistry students), is a chemical compound with the formula C_2H_5 (or $_6$)O - a flammable, volatile, colourless liquid with a vague characteristic aroma. It's the intoxicating ingredient in all alcoholic drinks, from beer to cider, to whisky to wine. The processes by which raw ingredients are converted into the finished product you get off the supermarket shelves are varied, although as a basic rule ethanol is produced naturally by yeasts that break down sugars. Ethanol mixes with water easily and is effective at killing microorganisms - which is why those hand sanitizers you've been using throughout 2020 contain alcohol.

To be clear, alcohol is a psychoactive drug - one that alters the mind. Yep, if you didn't know already, you're reading a handbook about a drug. Alcoholic beverages are (and should be) enjoyed because of flavours, relaxing qualities and social benefits. Alcohol is available on a massive global scale, although some countries either ban it, enforce regional bans, or have limitations on its sale. Its economical value is vast, perhaps too large to comprehend (we're talking about thousands of billions of dollars).

The effects of alcohol consumption are varied, including:

- Increased heart rate.
- Expansion of blood vessels.
- Increase in talkative / social functions.
- Lowering of inhibitions / slower reaction times.
- Impairment of decision making / judgement and co-ordination.

> *Consumption of alcohol can also bring false claims of you being the funniest person in the room. More often that will not be the case.*

Alcohol is both a stimulant and a depressant - the latter prominent in higher alcohol consumption, producing calming effects and stupor. Indeed, renowned author Anthony Burgess admitted that the comforting qualities of booze helped him write his most famous novel: "I had to write *A Clockwork Orange* in a state of near drunkenness," he said, "in order to deal with material that upset me so much." Which begs the question: why did he write it, then?

Alcohol affects the mind, whether the result is good or bad. There is no glossing over the fact that some appalling actions have been caused by drinking - these actions are often the sole responsibility of the guilty party. But let's not dwell on horror stories. Booze has produced great outcomes - of course - with several poets, writers, politicians, philosophers (and millions more individuals) profiteering from alcohol's valuable assets. What better to collect one's thoughts than a beer? Sure, a coffee and solitude may have similar effects, but an "illicit" alcoholic beverage could produce creative fireworks. Every now and again, booze is the only thing that triggers a moment of clarity. It remains obvious that the effects of alcohol are identified more in higher concentration - with age, gender, socio-economic status and genetics all seen as "vulnerability factors".

The above information is simply fact. Billions of people around the world enjoy a tipple with no major repercussions. Drinking is a wonderful activity if done responsibly (as it can if done irresponsibly). But, in all truth, most students are not particularly experienced in the drinking culture, despite many claiming to be so. A lot of students are too young to be proficient at drinking, so the dangers are higher in those who are "wet-behind-the-ears". If you've had minimal encounters with alcohol, the general advice before stepping through the campus doors is to go easy, and respect it.

Before term starts, it's advantageous if you've already experienced the delights of drinking. Having a pre-university social life holds many a student in good stead, because the progression to authentic student is smoother than those who are unskilled in the art of drinking. "Amateur" drinkers could find student life too full-on in the first few weeks, and they shouldn't be pressured into any drinking behaviour with which they're not comfortable. Be strong, be in control, be sensible. Going "too hard" will only end in failure - or worse. If you're scared of heights, your initial fear wouldn't be overcome by conquering a 10-metre diving board - you'd start with a three-metre one. The same rule applies with drinking. Easy does it...you'll get there in the end.

The act of being (or getting) intoxicated is prevalent throughout the world. This isn't to glamorise drinking; again, this is a fact.

However, there are thousands of millions of teetotallers who don't, won't or can't consume alcohol. Everyone's different. The French are renowned for partaking in beverages at an early age (e.g. early teens sampling wine at the dinner table), and many Europeans favour boozing in moderation (contradictorily, many European nations also excel in drinking). As mentioned, any prior participation in drinking is sure to be advantageous. The trick is to know your limits, and not to succumb to social pressures.

Chapter 2: Freshers' Week - what it is, what to expect, and what to do

With the effects and warnings of boozing out of the way, let's concentrate on what might be expected of you as a student, and what might happen in the days leading up to your first academic term.

The main event is Freshers' Week - "fresher" being a new student at university (short for "freshman", a term widely used in North America). It occurs in the days before the first semester kicks off, and is a chance to get acquainted with other lost sheep.

Freshers' Week is considered a vital grooming period - serving as a time for students to settle into university life. There are usually clubs and societies to join (or ignore), and in general Freshers' Week serves its purpose. But for many, the main purpose is to meet new friends over a few drinks.

Like the first day at a new school, Freshers'

Week is normally crammed with clueless students not knowing what's really going on. This is normal. Don't fret; if you did know what the norm is, they'd be something wrong.

What to expect during Freshers' Week

1. Confusion.

2. Terror / panic / fear. "Christ, what have I done?"

3. "Freeeedom!"

4. A thirst coming on.

5. At least one student hoping to "find themselves." Yuck.

6. Forms to fill in - these can wait, although registration is pretty important (after finding the Student Bar, of course - see below).

7. Advice on preparation. Prepare for this by ignoring it. There is no preparation; learn by your mistakes.

8. Stories of "Freshers' flu" - a somewhat childish "symptom" associated with

acclimatising to new surroundings. If suffering from this, talk to somebody and don't bottle it up.

9. Homesickness pangs. Natural, for sure, but they'll soon disappear after the first pint, much like the aforementioned "Freshers' flu".

10. Job offers from desperate companies needing bar staff because they've just realised summer is over and it's actually September.

11. Scout leader types keen to sign up students for societies and clubs, from "The Rock-Paper-Scissors Fan Club" to "The Jam Maker's Appreciation Society". Best avoided, unless you really are an enthusiast of fruit preserves. And just think of the time you'll save yourself when you want to unsubscribe! Drinking clubs are recommended, although the novelty will soon wear off.

What to do during Freshers' Week

✓ Locate the Student Union bar - you'll make new friends in no time - and commit to memory its co-ordinates.

✓ Find your nearest campus bar, as it'll feel more like a local than the Student Union. Plus, getting to know the bar staff gives you an edge over the rest of the pack. Never underestimate a barman's local knowledge or a barmaid's insights; use them to your advantage. They are your friends.

✓ Locate the nearest shop.

✓ Don't forget your wallet - buying the first round will make you a hero.

✓ Take any leaflet or flyer advertising cheap drinks or offers on booze. It's common sense, and even if you haven't connected with a similar-minded boozing chum on your first day, you can be sure that the advertised drinking establishments will be a good place to meet new friends in a similar situation.

Joe varley

✓ *Don't panic!* Everyone's in the same boat, just as they'll be in the same pub.

> *Locate your student accommodation quickly. The more belongings you ditch at your digs, the easier it'll be to seek out the nearest bars.*

✓ Write down your room number and full address and keep it safe, or store them in your phone. You'll thank yourself after your first night when you may not remember which postcode you're in.

✓ Make as many new boozing contacts as possible. "Contacts", because your true friends won't be apparent in the first week or so; you'll make your real friends later on. However, it doesn't harm having phone numbers, addresses etc early on.

✓ Buy a super-big communal box of washing detergent for your house / flat / floor of residence. It's a nice gesture, and you may even go the whole term without buying any more as your new pals reciprocate your act of kindness. (Plus, it's not as if you're going out of your way - you can buy it when you go to the nearest shop to acquire booze).

✓ Of all the maps and directions and various hand-outs given to students, a map of the town centre with the best bars is the only one you'll need on the first day.

✓ Save the number of the cheapest taxi service in your phone.

✓ Save the number of the cheapest take-away in your phone.

✓ See if there's a "booze cruise" company that delivers alcohol...and save the number in your phone. It'll come in useful in the first few weeks.

✓ Make friends with the more experienced students. They know the score, and are usually friendly and sincere. Plus, they'll guide you to the best bars in the area, as well as the ones to avoid.

Being a student is exciting, opening doors for new experiences - and new bars. Congratulate

Joe varley

yourself on making it this far. Buy the ticket and enjoy the ride.

Chapter 3: Students' Unions, Student Halls

Student Unions

Think of these as the student's boozing home-from-home. Most often run by students, Students' Unions are largely dependable, free from pretence, and can provide invaluable advice. You'll most probably need to register to access it regularly, or simply show your student card. Don't be afraid to inquire.

It's perhaps the best "club" to get involved with, as it represents you - the student. Yes - that's YOU! Aside from cheap drinking nights at the bar (often referred to as the "SU Bar", or "SUB" in text-speak), the Students' Union presents a familiar environment in which every student should feel comfortable - especially propped up at the bar. Though you'll invariably find plenty of welcoming watering holes in town (several of which will become your "local" - see chapter 4), don't dismiss the Student Union as just a meeting place for students. It's much more than that.

If you take one thing from Students' Unions, it's that they often provide pretty good beer and generic spirits at superb discounts, as well as cheap food to get through a hangover before embarking on another boozing crusade. Similar to a barman, use it to your advantage. Take note of any "happy hours" and use them astutely - i.e. whenever they occur.

Students' Unions often host gigs, and these are worth checking out. Follow these boozing tips for an enjoyable and accident-free music event:

- If served in plastic pint glasses, take a long sip of your beer at the bar before joining the crowd. This will eliminate any unwanted spillage from the flimsy drinking vessel. Don't make the floor more sticky.
- Treat bouncers with respect; they are your chums, and no one comes out on top against doormen.
- Don't leave booze near amps or any other electrical equipment. The logic is self-explanatory.

- Don't miss the support bands; often they are local and need support. Also, there is usually more drinking time before the place gets really packed out.
- Don't smuggle booze in hipflasks or by any other means; you're not at The Ritz, so the booze should be cheap enough. Plus, you don't really want to get barred from the SUB - it's disrespectful and embarrassing. Save hipflasks for money-grabbing, corporate destinations.
- By all means question any advert for "live" bands. As opposed to what? A band specialising in air guitar?
- Students' Unions champion students, lending a voice to the whole student community. It is run by students, for students. Consider these advantages, and ask yourself if you can afford not to get involved:

1. Drinks are, invariably, cheap.
2. Clientele will usually be in your age

bracket.

3. If you really need a job, Students' Unions are a good start.

4. They schedule social events.

5. Think of them as your comforting big brother, offering advice and guidance.

6. When you've run out of baked beans, SU's often provide good-valued meals.

On a national level, have a gander at www.nus.org.uk. This is the website for the National Union of Students. Here you may find extra information, advice, and discounts on national products (e.g. food, drink), and links to the TOTUM* student discount card and app (*formerly the NUS Extra). Formed in 1922, the NUS has been an indispensable "Sherpa" to students, and continues its good work.

Student Halls

There is a good chance you'll be residing "in halls" for your first year. For many students, it'll be an opportunity to make a favourable impression. On the first night in your new barracks, it's advisable to place a large bottle of vodka / crate of beer in the communal kitchen, on which you've stuck a Post-it Note. The note should invite your new drinking companions to sample forthwith, and to relay which lovely person supplied the booze. Don't forget to include your room number. Any self-respecting drinker (or decent human being) will accept a drink and thank you for it. It's a great way of initiating conversation instead of shuffling from room to room, knocking on doors for an awkward introduction.

> *The phenomena that are "beer walls" (the accumulation of empties) is undoubtedly a loving reminder of consumption, though they're too passé for the 2020s. However, by all means keep empty wine and spirit bottles, as they can double up as vases, ornaments and candle holders. SLY Dog Rum bottles are perfect.*

Though your room will be just large enough to

Joe varley

accommodate a small hippo, take a moment out of your drinking schedule to think about its layout. Do you have a bed? Check. Table and wardrobe? Check. Inflatable chair? Optional. Booze storage? This is critical! Beer should be purchased in boxes, as they are easy to store (and it'll save you unnecessary trips to the shops). 100 cans or bottles take up a mere two square feet of floor space - ideal for long-term boozing. Don't keep booze bottles near windows; instead opt for a cool space with convenient access.

The communal kitchen is a great drinking place - probably the only place, except your room. You need to establish habits quickly, on which you'll be judged by fellow residents. Never label food: it may seem sensible, but it just annoys others. If your compatriots are on the same wavelength, staple foods like butter, bread and milk should "magically" appear once everyone accepts replenishing essentials is their own responsibility. Let nature work its course. Keep the kitchen clean, but don't go overboard: would you rather live in a tip with friends, or alone in a palace?

Drink is another beast. Don't put more than a few bottles in the fridge at any one time, as these items could be seen as "fair game", and they'll disappear quicker than shit through a goose. Experiment with your freezer; bottles can reach optimal drinking temperature in half an hour, and it'll encourage speedy boozing before they freeze completely - otherwise the fridge will do. Vodka and rum can be stored in the freezer, but keep it out of sight - behind a packet of peas is ideal.

Your halls will have communal showers. Save on drinking time by taking in a beer whilst showering.

Student Hall checklist:

- ✓ Use the Post-It Note booze gesture.

- ✓ Buy booze in boxes / crates.

- ✓ Keep booze away from windows.

- ✓ Don't build beer walls - it ain't the 1990s.

- ✓ Keep empty large bottles - after they've

been washed out.

✓ Don't label essential foods.

✓ Limit beer bottles in fridge.

✓ Use freezer to conceal spirits.

✓ Drinking in showers is satisfactory; smoking may prove futile.

Chapter 4: Out in the field

Ah, the first "proper" university night out! It's what dreams are made of. It's an experience many students anticipate with thunderstruck excitement, and rightly so. New pubs! New booze! New people! New…everything!

The first night out in your new surroundings is akin to an army recruit training exercise in hazardous woodlands: both require research, and both carry a certain amount of caution. Camaraderie also plays an important part, with individuals relying on fellow companions for support. There's a strong guttural feeling of the unknown, fluttering gastric butterflies soon to be replaced by combat-inducing adrenaline.

The first night is an experiment - an opportunity to visit as many hostelries as possible. Your new boozing buddies will consist of new-found drunks from your student hall, and there might be a Student Union Representative to conduct proceedings. The evening (or day if you're starting early) is intended to be an introduction to what your new surroundings have to offer. You'll call in at run-down pubs with spit, sawdust or a combination of the two, as well as nondescript boozers with as much charm as an unwashed jockstrap. Maybe you'll smooch into a glitzy bar as James Bond, only to leave as Mr Bean. Make no mistake - half the visited hostelries will be forgotten by the morning, but that's where your comrades-in-arms should dig deep and patch blurs together to form some sort of recollection. The purpose of the first university night out is to dip your toe into a range of drinking holes, and to come out intact. Variety is the key. It should be embraced.

Drinking in an unfamiliar territory requires teamwork, like wild dogs hunting in packs. There should be no "mob mentality" hell-bent on disorder - more an assembly of merry men sussing out drinking options. Disorder and mishap might come later…

The first night on the lash can be a mixed bag. There'll be memorable successes and spectacular failures, or spectacular successes and memorable failures. They'll be spillages, tears, high jinks and losses (money, clothes, friends, dignity). Take them all in your stride. You're new to the area. Don't be too hard on yourself, or your companions.

There are over 160 "higher education" institutions in the UK (roughly), spread out in every corner. This geographical range, naturally, accounts for a diversity of drinking establishments. For students in larger cities, you may have to cast your drinking net wide to find the best boozers. In London, there could be more pubs and bars in a square mile on your doorstep than in a small university town. Larger cities like Manchester, Leeds, Glasgow, Newcastle and Sheffield are all renowned for their nightlife, so there'll be more pub research to be done here than in, say, Chichester.

Local knowledge is helpful when electing your pubs. Whilst your favourite boozer may very well be the one you blindly stumble into - unaware of its reputation or qualities - talking

Joe varley

with locals can pay dividends. Taxi drivers and shop owners are valuable assets, who will be only too glad to voice their recommendations. Ask and listen!

After the first few nights out, your boozing radar should be warming up. Your ears prick up at the words "drinks discount", "student's night" and "dirt cheap". You'll get to know your way around, and which pubs are the most suitable for students. This is called learning, and you'll soon be an expert.

An average small town in the UK might have a handful of pubs - let's say 15 for a town with a population of 15,000. If that town has links with a university or large college, the number of pubs is likely to be higher - perhaps doubled. Students buy alcohol, see. Students need pubs, and pubs need students. Most, anyway (see below).

Let's take The University of Wales, Aberystwyth, as an example (the birthplace of Zymurgorium Gin!). This Welsh seaside town is a hotbed of boozing opportunities.

Pubs close down, re-open, get re-branded and everything in-between, so it's futile to accurately keep up with how many boozers each place has - particularly in larger cities. That said, Aberystwyth is a modestly-populated town with an eye-catching amount of pubs. The town has around 17,000 inhabitants, and when uni is in full swing, the population increases by about 40%. With fluctuating student numbers (and with the economy having a far from 100% stability), numbers of pubs vary.

When on a night out, students often quickly develop a sixth sense in choosing local boozers. Décor is usually not important. In fact, a lot of students define pubs with character as those that lack plush environs. Generally, students appreciate good value and welcoming staff, and rebuke at pretence. Sticky carpets and chipped walls might deter some, but to most students these qualities are irrelevant. Range of drinks, solid staff and assorted facilities trump any flooring, expensive wallpaper or marbled toilets.

Joe varley

JD Wetherspoon

The first Wetherspoons opened in Muswell Hill in 1979 and has risen both in size and stature, continuing to be the UK student's favourite pub chain. Wetherspoons should be regarded by every student as their "go-to" pub chain. Consider the following:

Wetherspoons pubs are unique - each pub carpet is individually designed to reflect the history of the pub and surrounding area.

Apps can be downloaded and used to order food and drink.

All pubs maintain faultless hygiene standards in a comfy environment.

The fantastic selection of drinks and food offer the best value for the average student.

Can't find a Wetherspoons near you? You're not looking hard enough, as there are over 900 UK locations.

Treat Wetherspoons pubs as your faithful friend, and you won't go far wrong.

When "in the field", be wary of pubs that don't welcome students. It's difficult to fathom, but some pubs regard students as trouble makers and simply refuse them service. Indeed, some pubs might shun non "locals". Knowledge and experience play a key role in establishing which pubs to avoid. Plenty of pubs proudly display national flags, and whilst most of them are irrefutably hospitable, a handful can have prejudices towards customers of assorted backgrounds.

On the lash checklist:
Do:

- ✓ Visit lots of pubs. Obviously.

- ✓ Drink in groups during the first few dummy runs.

- ✓ Identify booze deals.

- ✓ Try local ales, if only to tick them off your beer list.

- ✓ Uncover pubs with pool tables, juke boxes etc.

✓ Ask for local recommendations.

✓ Discover pubs that host gigs (avoiding air guitar acts).

✓ Be wary of pubs flying national flags.

✓ Learn from mistakes.

Don't:

X Ignore research.

X Play the fool in front of police.

X Be casual in infamous pubs. You're on their turf.

Chapter 5: Beer - a student staple

"Milk is for babies. When you grow up, you have to drink beer." Arnold Schwarzenegger

"Beer…Now there's a temporary solution." Homer Simpson, Fox BC

Perhaps the most satisfying English word, when its letters are correctly arranged, is "beer". The word is simple, modest. It doesn't want for anything. It's easy to remember. It's dependable, solid, affable. Beer is a comfort blanket, and should be considered as the student's principal drink of choice.

> *Beer has humble beginnings. Though its origins are somewhat sketchy, beer is generally considered to have been "discovered" about 9,500 years ago in Mesopotamia (Iraq and surrounding areas).*

Our ancestors weren't stupid. They quickly hit on the idea of mixing grains with water, then adding yeast to produce a beery prototype.

Throughout the years - with more science added to the process - brewing became widespread. This natural procedure starts with fermentable sugars being extracted from grains using hot water. The liquid is then heated, and hops added for flavour. When cooled, yeast is added and fermentation commences - converting the sugar into carbon dioxide and alcohol. Hey presto - you have beer! Along with the wheel, electricity and the Web, beer is one of man's greatest discoveries - it's certainly one of the most useful.

> *People who are moderate consumers of beer have a 30-40% reduced risk of coronary heart disease compared to teetotallers. The World Health Organisation has described this as the "most important health benefit of alcohol."*

There are various systems that take place along this most critical of journeys: malting, milling, mashing, and conditioning. With a few tweaks, different types of beers are produced, all with varying alcohol by volume (ABV) strengths. Common types of beer are:

- Ales & bitters - often cask-conditioned, these are usually copper or bronze in colour, due to the use of dark malts. ABV is typically 3-4.5%.
- Lagers / Pilsners - light-coloured and extremely popular, usually fizzy with bubbly heads, stored at a cool temperature. ABV is usually 4-6%.
- Stouts & porters - a beer with a long history, barley is roasted at high temperatures to produce a dark brew, often with a coffee / chocolate flavour. Hops are added for bitterness. ABV is varied, though the 4-8% bracket is the norm.
- Wheat beers - common in Germany, Belgium and The Netherlands, high levels of wheat are mixed with barley malt to produce a crisp - and often potent - brew. Expect ABV to be higher than 4%, up to anything approaching 8% - and beyond.
- American ales - Popular due to the US craft beer movement, these are

Joe varley

aromatic, highly-hopped beers with varying colours. Highs of 7% ABV are not uncommon.

All five types are glorious.

Real ale - it's "live"

CAMRA (Campaign for Real Ale) has sought to clarify the definition of "real ale" for today's drinkers. Indeed, they've captured the common thread of all forms of "real ale" in a new definition of "live beer", which is "any beer that when first put into its final container contains at least 0.1 million cells of live yeast per millilitre, plus enough fermentable sugar to produce a measurable reduction in its gravity while in that container." One for the science students.

CAMRA's definition of a cask-conditioned beer is "a live beer that continues to condition and mature in its cask, any excess of carbon dioxide being vented such that it is served at atmospheric pressure."

IPA

IPA stands for "India Pale Ale" (not "Indian"!), and it largely launched the craft beer movement. No one really "invented" IPA; it evolved over centuries.

There are records of pale ale being consumed in 1717. It's customary to assume the beer that would become known as "IPA" evolved from "October ales" - brewed for storage and therefore possessing high hop and alcohol contents.

Pale ale was shipped to British troops stationed in India, and in order to preserve the beer during months at sea, the beer was given more hops and had a higher ABV.

TOP STUDENT BREWERY

Located under the shadow of famous Ilkley
Moor, this gem of a brewery is home to
some of the finest ales Yorkshire has to offer,
although their beers are sold nationwide.
Ilkley Brewery has an outstanding reputation,
using a variety of UK and worldwide hops and
malts to produce IPAs, session pales, Yorkshire
bitters, American pale ales, lagers, stouts and
low-alcohol beers.

Ilkley Brewery has always adopted an
innovative style of brewing, and they often
formulate beers with a nod to the region's
history. Take Hendrix - their 4.9% American
pale ale which was created in 2017 to celebrate

the 50th anniversary of guitarist Jimi playing in one of the town's hotels.

Need hand pumps and beer for parties or events? Of course you do - you're a student. No problem - the brewery hires the pumps, so students can celebrate a pub atmosphere in the comfort of their own digs.

Star beer - Mary Jane ("Yorkshire's Most Wanted")

- ABV: 3.5%
- Taste: 10
- Value for Money: 10
- Drinkability: 10
- Overall Student Rating: 10

Go to www.ilkleybrewery.co.uk for core beers, along with seasonal and special

brews. They also have a selection of T-shirts, hoodies and beanies. What's not to like?

There are more brands of beers - and indeed of any alcoholic beverage - than can be kept track of. A beer's availability - particularly ales and bitters - might be dependent on the region or, at least, regional popularity. Go with the flow, be responsible, and enjoy. As the Egyptian proverb states, "The mouth of a perfectly happy man is filled with beer."

Beer tips:

- Try as many as you can, but persevere with the brands and styles that work best for you.
- Some "sister beers" of the same brand may vary in strength - don't get caught out.
- High strength beers like Tennent's Super and Special Brew have their place but, like superhero powers, they should be used sparingly.
- A lime wedge in a beer bottle is poor

form. Unless you're in Mexico. Which you're not.

- Last night's Newcastle Brown Ale at 9am probably tastes as bad as it smells.
- Last night's Newcastle Brown Ale at 9.02am definitely tastes as bad as it smells.
- Most lagers need to be consumed cold.
- Wear coats with deep pockets if you insist on swigging from a beer can in public; a quick transfer to the aforementioned pocket will put police off the scent.
- Never correct a barman, even if they are wrong.
- Don't be too fussy about the type of glassware when drinking beer. The beer won't give a shit, so neither should you.
- Look into CAMRA. It's like the Bible, only useful.
- Guinness is lovely, thank you very much.
- There is no "right" way to drink beer, other than via your mouth.

- Low alcohol beers are student-friendly, honestly. Try Skinny Lager or Ilkley Brewery's Virgin Mary.

Chapter 6: Cider - fizzy goodness

"An apple a day keeps the doctor away, but buy him a cider and he'll be your friend forever." Anon

If beer is the student's principal drink, cider is not too far behind.

> *The UK consumes more cider than any other country. Hardly surprising, really.*

Brits love cider, and students aren't too diplomatic when demonstrating their affection for it. Cider strengths vary, although they tend to be at the higher end of the "blotto scale" (ABVs approaching 9% are not exceptional). In fact, when students reflect on past glories, cider is often the chief culprit.

Definitions vary throughout the world, too, but for the purpose of the everyday student, cider is made from the fermented juice of apples. Apples that produce the best ciders are known as…wait for it…"cider apples". When extra sugar (or fruit) is added before a second fermentation, the ethanol content increases. CAMRA's definition of "real" cider is that the drink must be made from the juice of freshly pressed apples - not syrup - and must be free from pasteurisation or artificial carbonation. Real cider, for sure, is not fizzy. This is obviously not seen in many brands, which are especially fizzy and achieve a solitary objective: to get the drinker pissed. K cider is a prime example.

The UK produces, roughly, 700 million litres of fizzy fruity goodness annually - that's a lot. The two geographical areas where cider features prominently are the West Country and East Anglia / South East. Herefordshire, with its vast number of orchards, is usually regarded as the no.1 UK county for cider.

A popular summer tipple for outside boozing, cider is ubiquitous in beer gardens throughout the land. Many drinkers perennially stick to cider, though the drink is probably not as popular in the colder months. That said, many manufacturers have supplemented the traditional apple flavour with more exotic tasting notes, like "berries & cherries", "kiwi & lime" and "pineapple & raspberry". The foundation is still apples, of course, but the current market dictated that adding more variety to ciders was always going to be a winner. Nowadays, "dark fruits" is as commonly seen in pubs as lager.

More so than beer, cider has the habit of sneaking up on the unsuspecting drinker, delivering its coup be grâce with cunning potency. Perhaps it's the sweet flavour that conceals its latent strength. Drink six pints of traditional Somerset cider and you'll be as pissed as a lord in a lock-in. Cider shouldn't be taken lightly - that's a given. Some may taste like an ice pop, but that's all the more reason to reserve respect.

Joe varley

With so many brands on the market, it's all too easy to opt for the cheapest, most bland cider. Instead, explore all your options and settle for your favourite. For example, try Sxollie cider, which crams in 3.3 apples per bottle. Sxollie is South African, too, which makes the cider the perfect choice for the student on the look-out for a cider just that little bit different.

Cider tips:

- Unless advised specifically, cider should be cold. Cider snobs will argue that extreme cold impairs flavours. Maybe so - but you're not a cider snob, right?
- Cider is ideal in house party punches.
- Relating to the above, supermarket bottles are invariably dirt cheap.
- Cider and radiators don't mix - keep cider in your room away from heat or strong sunlight.
- Cider is a tremendous substitute for water when making ice.
- Drinking cider quickly after playing

sport (especially a game of squash) is both refreshing and satisfying.

- Drinking cider quickly before playing sport (especially a game of squash) is both refreshing and foolhardy.
- Drinking cider in plastic pint glasses is perfectly acceptable.
- Snakebites (you know what they are) are as lethal as the name suggests. UK legislation can be a grey area, although asking for equal amounts of cider and lager to combine the two is perfectly legal. Some landlords, however, keep a beady eye on this practice.

Chapter 7: Wine - booze for all seasons

"Ask not what wine has done for you, but rather what you are willing to do for some wine." Anon

"My only regret in life is that I did not drink more wine." Ernest Hemingway

Now, let's get this right. There's a lot of snobbery in the wine world. If you even have to use the term "in the wine world", you're already on the fast track to being an oenologist (wine aficionado / elitist), and that's not especially creditable for a student - never mind a genuine wine-lover. There is unquestionably a great deal to learn about wine, from varieties, growing conditions, geographical regions, maturation, vintages and labels, but students shouldn't get too bogged down with the particulars. Like all booze, wine should be enjoyed at rudimentary levels.

If you must have delusions of grandeur (e.g. impressing a date), knowing the basics can pass as a connoisseur. Remember the following facts and you'll be halfway to becoming a wine snob:

✓ The basic process of wine making is: "Yeasts feed on sugars in the grape juice, producing alcohol, heat and carbon dioxide, changing the flavours of the grape juice to those of wine."

✓ Don't describe a faulty wine as "bad" or "off" - call it "out-of-condition".

✓ Most of the world's vineyards are found in a temperate zone between 30o and 50o from the Equator.

✓ As of 2020, the world's highest vineyard is in Tibet.

✓ The vintage of a wine is no indication of quality; it simply refers to the year in which the grapes were harvested in a single year.

✓ When appropriate, use the word "umami" when referring to food matchings. It means "savoury", and is one of the five basic tastes, along with "bitterness", "saltiness", "sourness" and "sweetness".

✓ The most common grape varieties found in supermarket wine are Merlot, Shiraz / Syrah (see below), Cabernet Sauvignon, Pinot Noir and Malbec (reds)…and Sauvignon Blanc, Chardonnay, Pinot Grigio and Riesling (whites).

✓ The black grape variety Shiraz is exactly the same as Syrah. "Shiraz" is the word used in Australian wines (part of the "New World"), while "Syrah" is used in French wines (part of the "Old World"). Most other regions use either name.

✓ The black grape Malbec is popular in Argentinian wines.

✓ Pinot Noir is a very light red wine, because the grape skins are thin and tannin levels low.

✓ The word "Merlot" is derived from the French word "merle", meaning "blackbird".

✓ "Cru" is a French term meaning "growth",

used to refer to wine of a specific vineyard. It's often used in conjunction with a quality ranking - e.g. "Premier Cru" means "first growth".

✓ "Dry" is a common term, although all wine is wet. It simply means the wine is not sweet.

✓ "Reserva" is a legally defined term for Spanish wines that have received extra aging either in oak barrels or in a bottle (or both). They are usually better in quality. "Reserve" carries no legal definition.

✓ The word "appellation" is an officially designated place of origin - especially in France. It's not really a guarantee of quality; just a guarantee that the wine comes from the region stated on its label. Two examples of appellations are Médoc in Bordeaux and Côtes du Rhône in south east France.

✓ All sherry is non-vintage, as it's a blend of wine of varying ages, produced by the solera system.

You probably won't need more than these to pass as a wine snob. For the more unassuming students, the following pointers will be ample:

- ✓ Wine is made from grapes by fermentation.

- ✓ Fortified wines (e.g. port, sherry) usually contain more alcohol.

- ✓ Buy wine, then drink it.

Is it acceptable for students to drink champagne? If you can afford it, why not? Champagne is usually associated with celebrations because of its superiority and lavishness (and price). Drinking champers may be suitable for birthdays, passing exams, or winning on the fruit machine. If you fancy alcoholic bubbles but are on a tighter budget, drink Cava (Spanish sparkling wine) or Prosecco (Italian) - hardly anyone will notice the difference. However, if you want to impress, good Champagne often has hints of bread or biscuits - and even nuts and chocolate; the taste is not noticeably fruity, unlike the cheaper Prosecco and Cava.

Is rosé wine only for the ladies? Usually, but not necessarily. Rosé wine is revitalising and contains booze, so fill your boots. Like red wines, rosé wines must be made from black grapes, but they're fermented at a lower temperature. Like a lot of white wine, they make excellent spritzers.

Which wines go with certain foods? Err…all of them. What a stupid question.

Any wine, mixed with fruit juices and lemonade, is perfect for punches. When cider is added, it's a notoriously potent concoction.

Wine in a box? Why not? Most boxes contain three litres, which is four standard bottles. Wine on tap! Go for it.

Historically, plastic screw caps (instead of corks) equated to inferior booze. Times have changed. If nothing else, screw tops permit quick entry to the product, and saves time searching for the elusive communal corkscrew, which your friend Tom may or may not have used to clean his toenails. Good wine is good wine, regardless of the bottle's cap. Even "bad" wine is commendable, as long as you enjoy it.

Lamentably, a glass of wine does not count as one of your "five-a-day".

> *"Beer before wine, you'll feel fine; wine before beer, you'll feel queer."* *Or is it the other way round? Who cares - if you mix the grape and grain in substantial quantities, you're going to know about it. However, numerous reports suggest that consuming wine after beer proves the downfall of the majority of drinkers.*

General wine rankings

Red wine - standard

- ABV: 10.5-15%
- Tongue discoloration: 9
- Value for Money: 8.5
- Hangover Severity: 8.5 / 9
- Overall Student Rating: 8.5

White wine - standard

- ABV: 10.5-13%
- Value for Money: 8
- Hangover Severity: 8.5
- Overall Student Rating: 8.5

Cava

- ABV: 10-12.5%
- Value for Money: 7.5
- Hangover Severity: 7.5
- Overall Student Rating: 7.5

Prosecco

- ABV: 11-12.5%
- Instant effect: 9
- Value for Money: 7.5
- Hangover Severity: 8
- Overall Student Rating: 8

Champagne

- ABV: 12-13%
- Celebratory purpose: 9
- Value for Money: 4 - 7 (depending on brand)
- Hangover Severity: 8

- Overall Student Rating: 6

Port

- ABV: 16-20%
- Post meal rating: 9
- Value for Money: 6
- Hangover Severity: 8.5
- Overall Student Rating: 6

Sherry

- ABV: 15-22%
- Value for Money: 6.5
- Hangover Severity: 8.5
- Overall Student Rating: 5

Chapter 8: Gin and distillation

"The only time I ever enjoyed ironing was the day I accidentally got gin in the steam iron."
Phyllis Diller

Distillation - the process of separating components from a liquid by boiling and condensation. The most popular drinks produced by distillation are gin, vodka, whisky / whiskey, brandy and rum, and they are usually served in the UK via optics, measuring out volumes of 25 or 35 millilitres (a "shot"), depending on the pub.

If we take 25ml to be the standard shot measure, a 70cl bottle will yield 28 shots (14 doubles), whilst a litre will provide 40 shots (20 doubles). Sometimes simply referred to as "spirits" or "liquor", these drinks should be enjoyed in moderation, lest a drinker succumbs to the following:

- Irregular, yet witty, speech.
- Flushed cheeks.

- Warped vision.
- Inability to perform the easiest of functions.
- Unreserved and shameless memory loss.

Usually, seven double measures (14 single shots) of any spirit will produce in the consumer any manner of the above behavioural abnormalities. Spirits should not be used recklessly by any student - especially on the night before an exam. As with all alcoholic tipples, treat them with the highest respect.

Most spirits are distilled from grains, fruit or sugarcane that have gone through alcoholic fermentation, giving a typical ABV value between 35-45%, although this varies on either side of the spectrum. The term "moonshine" was used for illicitly-made high-proof spirits.

Gin

A general definition of this most English of spirits is "a neutral base spirit that has been flavoured with botanicals." To be called gin, it must have juniper as the main flavouring. "London Dry Gin" is dependent on the making process (the neutral spirit must be re-distilled in a pot still with juniper and other botanicals) and has nothing to do with geographical regions. The term "Dutch courage" is universally thought to have derived from jenever - a gin originating in The Netherlands. Gins are typically unaged.

Tonic water is the natural companion for a quality gin, its quinine content universally recognised. Quinine is a compound classed as an "antimalarial", although quinine by itself is not the recommended solution for malaria. A gin and tonic (three ice cubes and a wedge of lime or slice of lemon essential) should be looked upon with affection as the quintessential spirit-and-mixer combination. That said, try different mixers such as bitter lemon, lemonade or orange.

Gin has a distinguished and colourful history, but to say it has seen a rebirth of late is only half the truth. The fact is that gin has always been popular - with obvious reasons. Nevertheless, a 21st century boom has seen an influx of gin societies, gin bars, subscription gin clubs and a whole host of innovative distillers throughout the world. A quality gin remains a quality gin, no matter the producer, so gin's magnificent flavour is enough to place it as a student favourite.

TOP STUDENT GIN BRAND

Zymurgorium is Manchester's first craft distillery, having been the brain child of Aaron Darke - then a student at The University of Wales, Aberystwyth. Aaron donned his trusty lab coat and got to work on the complex formula of Zymurgorium at his student flat, not knowing where his ingenuity would take him - or his gin. Roll on a few years, and Zymurgorium is one of the most respected gins in the UK, and should be regarded as the student's no.1 gin brand of choice. It's refreshing to know some students give something back to the student drinking community!

The brand name is an amalgamation of "Zymurgy" (the study of scientific brewing) and "Emporium". Though gin is very much their speciality, Zymurgorium produce liqueurs and rum, and their distinctive recipe list should be a "go-to" place for gin-loving students up and down the country.

- ABV: 40-65%
- Value for Money: 10
- Flavour: 10
- Cocktail potential: 10
- Sipping potential: 10
- Overall Student Rating: 10

Check out www.zymurgorium.com and make every moment epic!

Three of the best:

FlaGINgo Pink Gin

Manchester Marmalade Gin

Realm of the Unicorn Gin Liqueur

Chapter 9: Vodka

"Trust me - you can dance."

Vodka

The versatility of vodka means it's been a student spirit favourite for decades - and rightly so. Like gin, vodka is essential in many cocktails and punches, and makes for a fine drink with several mixers - or simply "straight up" for those who remain true to tradition.

The origin of vodka is ambiguous. Place a Russian and a Pole in the same room to start a genial conversation about vodka's history, and expect a fight within the first minute. Though it's generally regarded vodka was created in the 8th or 9th centuries, "vodka" is derived from the Russian word "voda", meaning "water" / "little water". What can be accurately reported is that vodka was astoundingly popular in both Russia and Poland, and continues to be consumed in almost every bar and pub around the world.

Vodka can be produced anywhere in the

world. Raw materials used in its production include grains (e.g. wheat, barley, rye), potatoes and grapes. Vodka is often distilled in column stills, producing a strength of 95-96% ABV. After filtration, vodka is reduced using water to a bottling strength of around 40% ABV. Vodka is typically unaged.

Some useful words to know associated with vodka include:

- Krepkaya - Russian terms describing vodkas of at least 56% ABV.
- Osobaya - Vodka made using traditional Russian methods.
- Zwykly - Polish word for "ordinary" or "standard".
- Wyborowy - Polish word for "premium" or "choice".
- Luksusowy - Polish word for "luxury" or "deluxe".
- Vodka can be a sophisticated tipple, with many drinkers acknowledging subtle tastes and textures. Conversely, vodka is perhaps the most popular spirit

enjoyed with a wide range of mixers, from cola and other fizzy drinks, to fruit juices and tonic waters.

Vodka is often responsible for deceiving the drinker into thinking they do indeed look good on the dance floor…in fact, it's rarely the case.

TOP STUDENT VODKA BRAND

CRAFTED IN UNITED KINGDOM
DARK MARINA

Forget the corporate, mass-produced brands. For the discerning student vodka-lover, an independent distiller with a focus on quality is the best option. Dark Marina is an up-and-coming vodka brand with a multitude of flavours on offer, from raspberry and cherry to caramel and Blue Ice - a unique vodka with an ice candy flavour reminiscent of subtle bubblegum.

Owner Magdalena created Dark Marina in July 2019. Being Polish, her family knows a thing or ten about vodka, and they use fruit picked by their technologists to give drinkers a clear, refreshing flavour. Students shouldn't  stick to humdrum brands - variety is the key! Dark Marina is a vodka brand that is sure to rise up the ranks and become a student staple.

- ABV: 38%
- Taste: 10
- Value for Money: 10

- Cocktail potential: 10
- Overall Student Rating: 10

Go to www.darkmarina.co.uk or visit local shops to discover the wonderful world of vodka!

Chapter 10: Rum

"Rum is tonic that clarifies the vision, and sets things in true perspective." *Brian D'Ambrosio, US journalist*

Ah, rum. One of life's simple pleasures, and a much-loved element in any student's social armoury.

Close your eyes and allow your mind to focus on this most fragrant of spirits. Bliss, yes? Rum is easy on the nose, evoking exotic destinations, sun-soaked beaches and a general party atmosphere familiar with most students. Though scrumptious by itself, rum is a global ingredient found in hundreds of cocktails.

To be classed as rum, the spirit must be made from a sugar cane product (molasses - a thick, syrupy substance - is the most common, and must be diluted with water before fermentation and distillation). After distillation, some rums can be aged. White rum is the most popular style, and dark rums often have caramel to thank for their colour - several brands are aged in oak. Rum features heavily in the Hunter S. Thompson cult novel The Rum Diary. Well, *duh*.

There are many regional variations, although rum can be broadly classified into three sections:

- Golden / Spiced rum - Golden rums are often smooth due to oak ageing. Superior brands have complex and intense aromas - think toffee, banana, coconut etc. Spiced rums are typically golden rums with the addition of spice flavourings, resulting in a deliciously fiery product.
- White rum - A popular style, most white rums are distilled to a high strength. Most are neutral in colour, and lighter in intensity to spiced rums. Some white rums are aged in oak, then deprived of their colour by charcoal filtration.
- Dark rum - Sweet, full-bodied and with hints of dried fruit and spice, dark rums often have their colour determined by

the addition of caramel. Superior dark rums are aged in oak for years.

The spices and aromas in rums are often guarded, instead allowing the consumer to drift away in a pleasant haze of alcohol without knowing exactly which flavours contribute to the rum's characteristics. With this in mind, students should try different varieties before coming up with a "shortlist" of favourites.

TOP STUDENT RUM BRAND

SLY Dog Rum should be at the top of rum choices as the preferred brand for students. It's made by a young, innovate team - recent university graduates - that places an emphasis on using the highest quality, 100% natural ingredients. A blend of premium Caribbean rums chosen from distilleries in the Dominican Republic and Jamaica (can you visualise the sun-soaked beaches yet?), SLY Dog can be quaffed straight up, or used in a whole host of cocktails.

- ABV: 40%
- Value for Money: 10
- Flavour: 10
- Cocktail potential: 10
- Sipping potential: 10
- Overall Student Rating: 10

Join the spiced rum revolution by visiting www.slydog.co.uk

Chapter 11: Other spirits

Whisky / whiskey

"Whisky is liquid sunshine." *George Bernard Shaw*

Generally, "whisky" is used for *Scotch* (Scottish whisky), whilst "whiskey" is used for any product other than in the land of the tartan - e.g. Ireland, USA etc. A basic definition of whisky is: "Oak-aged spirits made from grains such as rye, corn and barley." *Bourbon* is a term describing American whiskey made from a mixture of grains, although it must contain 51% minimum of corn - producing a slightly sweeter taste. *Scotch* whisky must be distilled and aged in oak casks in Scotland for at least three years. *Single Malt* Scotch is a malt whisky that comes from *just one distillery*. Blended whisky is usually a mixture of malt and grains, and tends to be inferior in quality to single malts. Irish whiskey is generally made from a mixture of malted and unmalted barley and is often unpeated, producing a lighter / smoother flavour than Scotch.

- ABV: 40-45%
- Value for Money: 7.5
- Hangover Severity: 9.5
- Overall Student Rating: 8

Brandy

Brandy and cigar, anyone? This is a spirit made by distilling wine (grapes), most of it aged in oak barrels and coloured with caramel before bottling - hence its sumptuous amber-brown hue. A traditional Christmas tipple. Cognac comes from the French commune of the same name - north of Bordeaux - and must be double distilled in a copper pot still. Armagnac is produced in the French region of the same name and typically possesses dried fruit aromas from column stills (as opposed to pot stills, used in Cognac production).

- ABV: 35-50%
- Old school rating: 9
- Value for Money: 7
- Hangover Severity: 9.5
- Overall Student Rating: 7

> *Letters on labels refer to the brandy's age: "VS" is "Very Special" and must be at least two years old; "VSOP" is "Very Special Old Pale" and must be at least four years old; "XO" means "Extra Old" and is a minimum of six years old.*

Tequila

A party drink and ingredient in many sophisticated cocktails. According to the Wine & Spirit Education Trust, tequila must be produced from 51% blue agave plant in the delimited Mexican region Tequila. "Blanco" or "silver" tequilas are for many the most authentic, with "Oro" or "gold" being unaged tequila with added caramel to soften the flavour. *Mezcal* is distilled from any species of agave (unlike tequila, which must be derived from the blue agave plant, *Agave tequilana*). Salt and lime is commonly taken before and after consuming tequila, although purists deride this practice. For "tequila hardman / stuntman" rituals, see next chapter.

- ABV: 40-45%
- Propensity to dance: 9
- Ability to dance: 6.5
- Value for Money: 8 (9.5 on "tequila nights")
- Hangover Severity: 9
- Overall Student Rating: 8

Perhaps more than any type of booze, spirits are the guilty party for memory loss (although three bottles of wine will have something to say about this). Another phenomenon attributed to spirit consumption is the "fresh-air sniper" - the affects of fresh air catalysing with alcohol in the bloodstream, resulting in the drinker falling over when stepping outside. The fresher the air, the worse the condition. Fresh air - add it to the list of drinking hazards...

Do:

✓ Be careful when mixing spirits.

✓ Try different cocktails.

✓ Try tequila without the customary salt and lime.

✓ Try different mixers to find your favourite drink.

Don't:

X Underestimate the ABV values.

X Fall victim to the "fresh-air sniper".

X Assume a bar is cool just because they have a gin menu.

Chapter 12: Shots and cocktails - the weekend starts here

"Dear alcohol,

We had a deal: you were going to make me funnier, sexier, more intelligent and a better dancer. I saw the video - we need to talk."
Anon

Shots are the equivalent of an alcoholic espresso: a quick pick-me-up before resuming with the pints or wine. Sure, you could have a whole night on shots, but it eliminates the social aspect of talking whilst drinking. Shots are useful in crowded bars, however, as you can have one whilst waiting for your round. Also, several bars have shot trays, making carrying a handful of delicious booze simple.

Many student bars also tempt customers with offers - if you've done your research you'll know which are the best ones. Shots are traditionally popular on Fridays and at the weekend - they're a true party drink and should be used almost as a "treat".

The following are some of the most popular drinks used as shots:

Sambuca

Sambuca is usually colourless, and has an unmistakable cough syrup-like aroma (it's actually anise / aniseed). Coloured varieties are common, and traditionally it's drunk with coffee beans, but unless you find yourself in Chelsea or Notting Hill, don't bother with them. Sambuca can be ignited, just to make drinking it more dangerous - it's often been blamed for burnt lips, tongues and eyebrows.

- ABV: 40-45%
- Value for Money: 8.5
- Hangover Severity: 8.5
- Burnt lip rating: 8 (9 if you're a rookie)
- Overall Student Rating: 8

Tequila Hardman / Stuntman

A curious practice performed by audacious drinkers looking for something different… and risky. Was it invented by Steve-O from

Jackass? Procedures are debated, but the general guide is: "Hardman" involves snorting tequila; "Stuntman" involves snorting a line of salt, downing a shot of tequila, followed by squirting juice from a lime wedge in your eye. It's irrelevant which of the two definitions is correct - both are ludicrous and likely to get you thrown out of a bar (watch out for the "fresh-air sniper" - he has you in his sights.)

- ABV: 40-45%
- Eye sore rating: 10
- Value for Money: 8.5
- Hangover Severity: 9
- Nose damage rating: 8.5
- Memory loss rating: 9.75 / 10
- Overall Student Rating: 7.5

Jägermeister

Hailing from Germany and meaning "master hunter", Jägermeister is a cult hero in student drinking circles. Regarded as a *digestif*, "Jäger" contains 56 herbs and spices and the bottle is as instantly recognisable as its taste and smell. The now ubiquitous "Jägerbombs" (a shot dropped into an energy drink) are fantastic for "oomph" and sticky lips.

- ABV: 35%
- Waiting at the bar beverage: 9
- Value for Money: 8.5
- Hangover Severity: 9
- Overall Student Rating: 9

Absinthe

When drinkers ask if a drink is legal, that's all you need to know. Absinthe will get you in the end - it always does. It *is* legal (as of publication date), although bar managers treat it with the notoriety of the Bubonic plague. Indeed, it's simply not stocked in a lot of pubs. It's nicknamed the "green fairy", largely because it's green and you'll make friends with fairies after a few shots. Vincent van Gogh enjoyed the beverage more than most, and he cut off his ear after a tiff with Paul Gauguin - the artist suffered from hallucinations, so absinthe's wormwood effects probably didn't help his cause. The buffoon.

In 1905, Jean Lanfray was committed of murdering his wife and two children after drinking absinthe. Never mind he also consumed seven glasses of wine, six glasses of Cognac, a brandy-laced coffee and two crème de menthes...

- ABV: 45-75%
- Value for Money: ? Decide for yourself
- Hangover Severity: 9.5
- Overall Student Rating: N/ASchnapps

Miscellaneous alcoholic beverages that take several guises, from fruit brandies to spiced herbal liqueurs. Usually sickly sweet. Frequently classified as a lady's drink and often found in cocktails.

- ABV: 15-40%
- Sweet tooth: 8
- Value for Money: 7.5
- Hangover Severity: 8
- Overall Student Rating: 7

✳✳✳✳✳

Cocktails conceal their true potency, often

tasting like they contain no booze at all. Most student bars will have their own cocktail names, with ingredients etched on a blackboard. For accepted cocktail recipes, visit www.iba-world.com (International Bartenders Association) for glorious concoctions.

For the best RTD (Ready to Drink) beverage, VK is the student's favourite and should be regarded as a vital party drink. For more information, visit www.globalbrands.co.uk. They also have some of the best tonics and mixers, so go wild!

Here are some cocktails you may come across in your student drinking career (some ingredients may vary, but the main booze constituent should be the same). All are perfect for making in student halls, at parties, or in drinking games.

- **Slow Comfortable Screw** - Vodka, orange juice, Southern Comfort, sloe gin.
- **White Gummy Bear** - Cherry vodka,

peach schnapps, pineapple juice, lemonade.

- **Kamikaze** - Vodka, orange liqueur, lime juice.
- **Screaming Orgasm** - Vodka, amaretto liqueur, coffee liqueur, Irish cream liqueur.
- **Sex on the Beach** - Vodka, peach schnapps, cranberry juice, orange juice.
- **Long Island Iced Tea** - Vodka, tequila, rum, gin, Cointreau, lemon juice, syrup, Coke. Best for value. 👍
- **B-52** - Kahula, Baileys, Grand Marnier (orange liqueur)
- **Slippery Nipple** - Baileys and butterscotch schnapps.
- **Irish Car Bomb** - Baileys and an Irish whiskey shot placed in a glass of Guinness.
- **Bloody Mary** - Vodka, tomato juice, lemon juice, Worcestershire sauce, Tabasco, salt, pepper, celery (optional). Best for hangovers. 👍
- **Screwdriver** - Vodka, orange juice.

Best for no imagination. ☺

Oh, the fun you'll have ordering some of these with a straight face - bartenders will have heard them all. Or, make one up yourself - e.g. adding peach schnapps and cranberry juice to the first cocktail will give you a "Slow Comfortable Screw on the Beach". Unless, erm, it's been done already, which it probably has. Sod it, make one anyway.

For gin-inspired cocktail recipes, be sure to check out www.zymurgorium.com/recipes

Chapter 13: Paying the price - how to get the best value

Drinking is an art, and requires certain skills. At some stage during student life, you'll want to have a few drinks when your bank balance is looking as healthy as three-week old lettuce. Don't give up! By exploiting the below suggestions you'll soon be speeding down the Super Booze Highway on minimal funds.

- **Homebrew.** Once the equipment and ingredients have been acquired, homebrew is a cheap drinking option. Excluding apparatus, a typical price per pint is anywhere between 20-60 pence. Starting with spotless equipment is vital. For homemade distillation (i.e. spirits), you need a licence, as you do with most hazardous practices.
- **Homemade wine ("Vin fait maison" / "Vino di blotto").** Relatively simple procedure involving grape juice, sugar and / or wine yeast. Kits are available. ABV values vary - some homemade

wine can be used to power small nations.

- **Avoid drinking bottles in bars**. You pay for the transportation costs, labels, advertising etc. The savings might not appear vast, but price per volume of beer is cheaper in pints.
- **Offers**. As previously recommended, scourge your university catchment area for the best deals and offers. Group taxis for farther-flung boozers advised.
- **Pre-going out drinks**. If you want to go out on a budget, the obvious proposal is to get partly-lashed on cheap booze before venturing out.
- **Use hip flasks**. Essential gifts for the professional drinker, though best used in places you dislike. Don't use hip flasks in your local, as it's disrespectful to your favourite bar staff and manager!
- **Kitties**. Indispensible if drinking on a budget. You'll be delighted with how far your combined money goes.

Operate a "beer piggy bank", saving pound coins from your spare change. Instead of wasting the coins on non-essential items like takeaways and magazines, you'll be staggered at how many alcohol units can be accumulated in a relatively short time.

Organise a quiz at your student digs. Collect a fiver from everyone and pocket £20 as your fee as the quizmaster, giving the remainder to the winner. It's like being a bookie, but more enjoyable.

- **Avoiding rounds**. Not for everyone (but everyone knows who does it). Best not to practice these in front of your "proper" mates, as it could end a beautiful relationship. Tried-and-tested avoidance tips include:

✓ Go for an extra long wee a few moments before your turn at the bar.

✓ "Er… hello? Is that the most important person I've ever spoken to?" Pretend to get an urgent call at the right moment.

✓ Enter the pub last, loitering at the back of the group like Billy No Mates.

✓ Did you lose your wallet? No? But the group doesn't need to know.

✓ Nip outside for three cigarettes, saying you "got chatting" upon your re-entry.

✓ If affordable, buy the first round in the hope that some might forget whose turn it is later on (everyone knows who *hasn't* bought a round).

✓ If your drinking companions are *real* friends, come clean and admit you're skint. We've all been there, and they'll probably come to your aid. The legends!

- **Bite the bullet.** WhatsApp your parents, asking for a little money, promising them it'll last longer than three days.

Chapter 14: Hangovers, units and the "What happened last night?" scenarios

Some drinkers don't get hangovers (yeah, right.) Others are committed to 48 hours in bed with a bucket as company. We're all different. One universal fact is that if you drink a lot of booze, you'll have at least one symptom of over-indulgence - however minor. It's simple science. After all, alcohol is a strong chemical compound and your puny body isn't wholly resistant against it.

> *Even legendary boozers get /got hangovers: it's neither big nor clever to feign them. Oliver Reed and Richard Burton surely had plenty. And Peter O'Toole. Oh, and Richard Harris. We're all human.*

What is a hangover?

In general terms, a hangover is the result of acute alcohol poisoning. It's the combined unpleasant effects of drinking too much booze

- both physical and physiological. Though hangovers have been observed for more than 3,000 years, the word itself was first used in the early 1900s (it's thought to have derived from an expression used in meetings for unfinished business).

Common hangover symptoms include:

- Headaches (perhaps the most frequent complaint).
- Sweating (antiperspirants are futile).
- Stomach cramps.
- Drowsiness (lack of "proper" sleep).
- Nausea (you have been poisoned, after all).
- Anxiety.
- Lack of appetite.
- Dry mouth ("like Ghandi's flip-flop.")
- Decline in concentration, coordination and awareness (though you'll be aware you've been drinking).

Why do we get hangovers?

Because you're a lightweight? No, actually.

The causes of hangovers are not as clear-cut as one would assume. However, scientific consensus dictates there are some reasons for this nasty condition. Let's look at a few of them:

- Hangovers usually develop when the blood-alcohol returns to zero (i.e. big hangovers won't arise when alcohol is still in your body). This is why a lot of people "wake up still drunk", and then feel worse a few hours into the day.
- The body breaks down methanol and ethanol into toxic formaldehyde, formic acid, and acetaldehyde a few hours after consumption - causing illness.
- Dehydration - the killer symptom. Alcohol decreases anti-diuretic hormone production, something the body requires to absorb water. Alcohol also makes you wee more, and your body needs to replace the liquid with something non-toxic.
- Alcohol affects the central nervous system.

Joe varley

- Blood sugar levels may decrease.
- Alcoholic metabolism can deplete vitamins and electrolytes.

Which drinks produce the worst hangovers?

Again, different people cope better with different drinks. However, if you feel particularly shredded after a night on the sauce, it'd be wise to avoid the type of drink which got you in the state in the first place.

A broad word of advice is to stick to lighter coloured drinks. Some people reel in horror at the smell of certain drinks (e.g. sambuca, whisky and tequila) simply because it evokes painful drinking experiences.

If you drink any type of booze in sufficient amounts, you probably won't escape hangovers. That said, try gin and tonics (fewer calories as well), vodka, white wine spritzers or fruit-based cocktails. It's a "suck-it-and-see"-type experiment, so go with it and discover for yourself.

Tips to avoid hangovers

- Listen to your body (if it answers you, you've got a hangover).

- Carbohydrates and fats usually reduce alcohol absorption, so eating foods like pasta before boozing *can* reduce the effects - though it's not foolproof. Drinking on an empty stomach is **not a good idea**; your body is likely to reject the booze later in the evening in the form of vomit. Not pleasant.

- Be wary of congeners in dark spirits - some people are sensitive to them. Congeners are natural chemicals (e.g. tannins and methanol) which can irritate blood vessels and brain tissue, increasing your hangover. They are found in booze like brandy and red wine. Generally, vodka, gin and beer have the least amounts.

Drink a pint of water before sleeping; this is not as easy as it sounds when you can't find the tap.

Joe varley

- Some people opt for fizzy drinks in-between boozy tipples which, though possibly scientifically wise, is a hassle and could cost you money in the long run. But it might be worth it - your choice, folks. Probably best to drink a few glasses of water.

Cigarettes and recreational drugs

Smokers may suffer from worse hangovers than non-smokers, and smoking probably does contribute to the dry mouth sensation. If you smoke, try to reduce your habit and see if you feel better the next day. It could be a coincidence, but maybe not. Who knows? If it works for you, stick to it.

Recreational drugs won't have any positive effect on hangovers - quite the opposite, in fact.

"Hair of the dog"

This is drinking booze (usually the same drink as the previous night) to reduce the effects of a hangover. In effect, it's killing a hangover with the booze that caused it - a vicious cycle.

Short for the expression "Hair of the dog that bit me", it was used by Jack Torrance in *The Shining* when he orders bourbon on the rocks from Lloyd - "the best goddamn bartender from Timbuktu to Portland, Maine - or Portland, Oregon, for that matter." It works - sort of - but only in the interim. The overall effect is you'll feel worse the day after, and the day after that...

Remedies to try

So, it's the day after, and you're feeling a little "delicate". Decay in bed in a festering mess, or brave the outside world? Go for the latter - force yourself, you *can* do it! It's a lovely feeling being the first person to emerge after a communal binge. Plus, you'll be seen as a drinker not to be trifled with.

The author has scrutinised some remedies from "real*" drinkers, which are highlighted below (*i.e. not fabricated). Some will work for you, others won't. The drinkers are credited - research trumps conjecture! Experiment with some of them - you might just find that all-important miracle cure. If not, stick to water, rest and abstinence for a couple of days.

- Angostura bitters (Jol Fitton).
- IRN-BRU, cold chocolate milkshakes with ice cream (Kyle Hamilton, James Hall, Bex Manson).
- Spicy Pot Noodle®, extra chilli oil (Paul Thomas).
- Reheated kebab, flat Coke left opened from the previous night (Fraser Farmery).
- Bovril, cigarettes (Matt Brown).
- Flat lemonade (Belinda McLeod).
- Vodka (Steve Prince).
- Salt & vinegar crisps, full fat Coke (Mandy Manson).
- Fry up (Andrew "Cheesy Chips" Maudsley).
- Blue Powerade, chicken pie (Henry Barrow).
- Pro Plus®, bacon butty, Coke (Sarah Oliver).
- 15-hour kip (Stephen "Hitch" Hitchen).
- Pint of lemonade with three raw eggs

(Mark "Thropy" Throp).

- Potato waffles, bacon, beans (Ewan "Cop Dog" Copsey).
- Cola ice pops (Bill Lever).
- Hash browns, IRN-BRU (Jasmine Thomson).
- Jalapeño hummus, Twiglets (Lindsay Fitton).
- Bloody Mary (John Hope).
- Diet Coke (Harriet Fairhurst).
- "Just deal with it!" Or Big Mac®, vanilla milkshake (Gus Rogers).
- Hot shower, hair dryer, tinned tomatoes on toast (Jayne Brearley).
- A trip to a bakery, then pub (Tim "Snakeman" McTigue).
- Full Scottish breakfast (Mark Hockey).
- Lucozade, salt & vinegar crisps (Ange Button).
- Dioralyte (James "Yazz" Davidson).
- Back to the pub (Matthew "Grimesy" Grimes).
- Flossing (Rob Manson).
- Two pints ("Rocking" Rod Hepworth).

- Heinz chicken soup (Mary Varley).
- Pork pie, HP™ sauce, two pints of lager (Will Golding).
- Fish finger sandwich, Coke (Amanda Lambert).
- Mushy peas (Ashleigh Murphy).
- Large G&T (Andy Steadman).
- Laps of Ilkley Cricket Club on a Sunday afternoon with Nick "Cocky" Cockcroft, plus beer (Jono "Boom" Hughes).
- Hot and cold shower (three hours), Lucozade (Alex Miller).
- Water, ice, lemon juice, lime, orange, frozen berries, honey (Adrian Curutiu).
- Spam, eggs, black pudding, cheese sandwich, Lilt® (Andrew "Rhodsey Lad" Rhodes).
- Kiwi fruit (James Fountain).
- Natural hangover aid: Cured.co.nz (Leighton Parsons, Kiwi legend).

From the selected above list, flat soft drinks are mentioned more than once. Fizzy drinks accelerate alcohol absorption, so there may be some truth in this. A "Full English / Irish / Scottish" is a common remedy, as fried food is good for quick fat and carbohydrate intake. But the bottom line is: if there was a 100% foolproof cure for everyone, it'd be manufactured, marketed and sold across the world (think of all the money for the patent!) But there isn't, otherwise it'd have been snapped up on *Dragon's Den*, so keep experimenting with remedies. Hopefully at least one of the above will prove beneficial to the student drinker.

How to deal with last night scenarios

10.38am.

Light is straining through the curtains. Congratulations, you made it to bed - maybe even your own. Or maybe you're lying in an allotment (you didn't make it to bed after all, but at least you can take home some carrots). It could be worse. You could be in a tree, locked up, or in the bear enclosure at the local zoo. Your eyes won't open, and you seem to have swallowed some super glue. All you know is that you're *sort of* awake.

An hour passes, your body telling you that you overdid it. The thought of food is abhorrent. You're in bad shape. And then the first inkling that something went amiss last night…a hazy, dark, horrible feeling that you may have committed a despicable act - one which demands an apology. Redemption is the only answer. But what the hell was it that you did? What exactly happened after the third shot of sambuca? Because that's sure as hell the last thing you remember: slamming down the shot of gloopy, aniseed devil's water after a gallon of ale. For a million quid you can't recall anything. Only that…you did *something* wrong.

For the sake of argument, let's say you got boisterous, fell over, and insulted your friend. Not the worst thing to happen, but it still warrants a "kiss and make up". How do you approach this? Follow these guidelines, and you'll soon be on your way to making things right with your pal:

- Don't dither in bed hoping it'll all go away.
- Get out of bed (or exit the allotment).
- Have a hot shower, followed by a cold one. Force yourself.
- Down a pint of water (ah, *there's* the tap!), or follow any of the above remedies.
- Go to the source: speak to someone who you think might know the particulars.
- Be honest. Relate your lack of memory to a friend, who may be able to fill in the blanks.
- If there is a cause for a sincere apology, hold up your hands and take the blame. Don't laugh it off. Fake guilt is a terrible quality; express your guilt and ask for forgiveness.
- Offer the offended party a gift / meal / drink. Don't grovel - just be sincere.
- More than likely, it'll be brushed under the carpet, and the two of you will be all-conquering booze buddies in

no time. You never know, your friend might be feeling bad about the episode, too.

- Stay clear of the type of booze that initially made you act like a sloppy, belligerent tosspot - opt for something else, and keep to it.
- Don't wallow in self-pity for too long. You're a student - shit happens. Try to learn from mistakes.

Units

In 1987 in the UK, some bright spark came up with a simple way for the competent drinker to keep track of their booze intake. Enter "units". Units are a way of expressing how much alcohol is in a drink.

One unit equals 10ml (or 8g) of pure alcohol, which is roughly the amount of alcohol the average adult can process in an hour. This means, *theoretically*, that within an hour there should be zero (or very little) alcohol left in the blood of an adult after drinking a unit of alcohol, although this will vary from person to person. Two bottles of wine (ABV 12%), for example, equates to 18 units, and therefore will take about 18 hours to leave your body. Units were likely to be thought of for health reasons, and to avoid being drunk when getting into a car in the morning. Obviously, the volume of drink and its ABV value dictates how many units are in said drink.

Guidelines seem to vary from year-to-year, although individuals are advised not to consume more than 14 units per week.

The table below illustrates popular drinks and their unit values:

DRINK	UNITS
Single shot of spirits (25 ml, ABV 40%)	1
Alcopop (275 ml, ABV 5.5%)	1.5
Small glass of wine (125ml, ABV 12 %)	1.5
Bottle of beer / cider (330ml, ABV 5%)	1.7

DRINK	UNITS
Can of beer / cider (440ml, ABV 5.5%)	2
Pint of beer (568ml, ABV 3.6%)	2
Standard glass of wine (175ml, ABV 12%)	2.1
Pint of beer / cider (568ml, ABV 5.2%)	3
Large glass of wine (250ml, ABV 12%)	3

Chapter 15: Effects on typing - *The Hitchhiker's Guide to Poor Coordination*

As a student, you'll probably do at least one of the following under the influence of alcohol / when hungover:

- Attend a lecture.
- Attend a practical lesson.
- Conduct research.
- Revise for an exam.
- Sit an exam.
- Type a "paper".

This is not advisable - just a good bet. We'll concentrate on the last item, and see how alcohol affects typing.

As discussed, alcohol decreases the ability to concentrate and to perform simple tasks, which some find difficult as it is when sober. Alcohol also dramatically reduces reaction time (one of several reasons why drink-driving is a strict no-no).

A sentence was chosen to show how error-free keyboard skills deteriorate with an increase in alcohol consumption. The "test" was undertaken in "laboratory conditions", with no outside influences or distractions - just 4.6% lager and a laptop (with occasional toilet and nicotine breaks).

The chosen sentence is taken from *The Hitchhiker's Guide to the Galaxy* by Douglas Adams. In fact, it's the very first sentence of the book:

"Far out in the uncharted backwaters of the unfashionable end of the Western Spiral arm of the Galaxy lies a small unregarded yellow sun."

After every drink consumed, the same sentence was typed from sober to eight drinks, resulting in the typing of the sentence nine times.

Though the effects of booze are undeniably affected by a number of factors (food intake, fatigue, type of booze etc), the exercise was conducted prior to eating and in optimal wellbeing. *Typing speed was uniformly maintained.*

Hopefully, one thing can be reliably deduced before the test: increase in alcohol units = decline in accuracy levels.

Round 1. Sober:

Far out in the uncharted backwaters of the unfashionable end of the Western Spiral arm of the Galaxy lies a small unregarded yellow sun. **Alcohol units: 0. Mistakes: 0.**

Round 2. After one beer:

Far out in the uncharted backwaters of the undashionable end of the Western Spiral arm of the Galaxy lies a small unregarded yellow sun. **Alcohol units: 1.5. Mistakes: 1.**

Round 3. After two beers:

Far out in the uncharted backwaters of the unfashionabee end of the Western Spiral arm of the Galaxy lies a small unregarded yellow sun. **Alcohol units: 3.0. Mistakes: 1.**

Round 4. After three beers:

Far out in the uncharted backwaters of the

unfashionable end of the Western Spiral arm of the Galaxy lies a small unregarded yellow sun. **Alcohol units: 4.5. Mistakes: 0** (Whaaaat?!).

Round 5. After four beers:

Far out in the unchartered backwaters of the unfashionable end of the Western Spirla arm of the Galxy lies a small unregarded yellow sun. **Alcohol units: 6.0. Mistakes: 3.**

Round 6. After five beers:

Far out in the unchartered backwaters of the unfashionabe end of the Western Su spiral arm of the Galaxy lies a small unregarded yeloow sun. **Alcohol units: 7.5. Mistakes: 5.**

Round 7. After six beers:

Far out in the unchartered backwaters of the unfasjionable end of the Western Sun Spiral arm of the Falaxy lies a small unregarded yellow sun. **Alcohol units: 9.0. Mistakes: 4.**

Round 8. After seven beers:

Far out in the unchartered backwaters of the

unfashionable end of the Western Spiral arm of the Galaxy lies a small unregared yerllow sun. **Alcohol units: 10.5. Mistakes: 3.**

Round 9. After eight beers:

Far out in the the uncharteed backwaters of the unfashinoanle end of the Western Sprila arm of the Galaxy lies a small unregarded ywllow sun. **Alcohol units: 12.0. Mistakes: 6.**

Bonus round. After eight beers and a cheeky gin & tonic:

Far out in the unchartr backwates of th un unfshonale end of the Western Spiral Sun arm of the Galaxy lies a small unregarded yelow sun. **Alcohol units: 14.0. Mistakes: 9.**

The results can be observed clearly in the graph below:

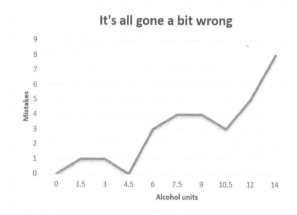

It's all gone a bit wrong

Conclusions:

1. The word "unfashionable" is tricky to type correctly with alcohol in one's bloodstream, possibly due to the spacing on the keyboard.

2. As are the words "unregarded" and "yellow".

3. Douglas Adams wrote sober...or had a sober commissioning editor.

4. Alcohol does not aid coordination, nor does it aid secretarial skills.

5. University work should not be undertaken with alcohol; save it for the post-work celebratory drinking.

Chapter 16:
End of Year Balls (up)

Thinking about spending £200 on a suit? Maybe you can afford that little red number you saw in the boutique shop in town. Perhaps you'll hire a tuxedo for the weekend, fully expecting to pay for the dry cleaning on the Monday morning. Maybe you'll tell Naomi at your Sport Science lectures you don't think she's the most wonderful person in the world and that she is, *in fact*, an obnoxious sycophant with the attributes of a turd. If you're thinking about these things, it's nearly time for the End of Year Ball, known as the "May Ball" in some circles.

Whatever it's called, it's normally labelled the "Big One", which is nonsense, since the average student drinker will have had much bigger nights out. But, however you look at it, just forget all the preparation you intend to put in - you'll wear the first suit you set your eyes on, and plan more on high jinks and booze. Gents - by all means find a nice suit, but leave it there - don't go overboard. For the ladies, it's understandable to go "all-out" on a dress, heels and matching purse: you'll look incredible. Really. Until you fall over.

Locations of the Annual Ball, of course, vary. If you attend a city university, it could be at a renowned Hall or hotel, or even on campus. For smaller, more rural universities, perhaps an out-of-town venue in a field has been chosen, complete with fairground rides and mud. Whichever one you attend you'll have a great time, but the following may hold you in good stead:

- Some universities publish handbooks re: May Balls. They might be constructive, although the emphasis on drinking tips will be slim.
- Don't forget to shower. You'll thank yourself when it's nearly midnight and you're sweating like Porky Pig at a butcher's sale.
- Choose your pre-drinks carefully. These are essential, and will gear you

up for the night's shenanigans. Light, delicate drinks like fruit-based cocktails or Prosecco will do nicely. As will cold beer. Sipping two cans of Tennent's Super is admirable, but will ultimately be your downfall.

- This is when you'll be grateful you received a hip flask last Christmas. They are the essence of any dedicated drinker's armoury, and will save you at least £20. Vodka or gin is preferable, as they'll mix well with unattended glasses of…well, anything.

- Make sure your phones are charged, and don't waste power by sending ridiculous texts before the real drinking starts. You'll need as much juice as possible to take the 387 photos you're planning.

- Buses - don't miss them. You'll only waste boozing time, and may have to pay for taxis - which would be a double whammy.

- Ladies (or men) - heels are your enemy.

More than two inches and you're asking for a tumble.

- Keep purses and wallets safe. Lots of accessories can be salvaged after a boozy night out, but when it's in the middle of a field or extravagant hotel, the chances of recovery are diminished.

- If you don't have a hip flask, bring with you a pocketful of miniatures. Say, rum.

- Don't pay for champagne. Okay, it's a celebration, but glasses could go for anything between £4-£10. Well, if can afford it, fill your boots. Otherwise, stick to your hip flask and the bar.

- Try to pay in cash. The dreaded contactless cards will ruin you the next day.

- Eat, but don't queue up - it's a waste of time. Fill up before you leave.

- If you really want to see the band who are booked to play, go ahead. There are plenty of quality, prominent bands who play at May Balls, as well as some lesser-known local bands, which can be just as good.

- If the Ball is at a hotel, the temptation to indulge in mischief is heightened: nicking food, pranking a paying guest etc. Be careful. Hotels have professional staff who have seen it all before, and may not turn a blind eye to such capers.

- Group photos - you may have to pay for them. If that's the case, it's your decision, though usually they're a waste of money.

- Don't get lost! If it's 3.47am and you're waddling in four inches of mud whilst wearing a bin liner and serenading a scarecrow, there are two sincere assumptions: 1. You're pissed. 2. You're lost.

- Dry cleaning. It doesn't matter if you've made a dress especially, hired a tux, bought a suit, or nicked a costume - budget the dry cleaning bill into your spending money.

Chapter 17: The UK's best boozing university cities / towns

The UK has some of the finest cities and towns for the discerning student (drinker) - you don't need a handbook to tell you that. A student's choice for their preferred university will be determined largely by the course and the university's teaching reputation - no question there - but the quantity and quality of drinking establishments is also an important factor.

Is there a North / South divide in the UK when it comes to boozing? Probably! There's certainly a difference in price, if nothing else…

The following cities / towns have been crudely ranked with the following criteria in mind:

- Quantity of pubs / bars (this consistently varies depending on the "ecological climate").
- Quality of pubs / bars (this changes, too, depending on the owners).
- Value for money.

- Drinking culture.
- Location.

(Apologies for the omission of any cities / towns: this ranking is merely a general guide).

"Gold standard" places to suit students of all tastes.

- **Manchester** - England's 3rd largest city, and one of the largest universities in the UK. Manchester's boozing opportunities are vast.
- **Newcastle** - Renowned *globally* for its nightlife, shenanigans, and cocktail offers. A boozer's paradise.
- **Leeds** - The 4th largest city in England, and growing all the time. Top UK university city, with plenty of boozing options. "The Otley Run" is legendary.

- **York** - Full of history, full of pubs. And only a short train journey to and from Leeds. A sure-fire winner.
- **Bristol** - Cider and craft beer feature prominently in this thriving South-West city.
- **Cardiff** - The Welsh capital champions a great range of boozing establishments within an easily accessible catchment area.
- **Liverpool** - Famed for its culture, Liverpool has the perfect blend of old-school boozers and contemporary bars.
- **Northumbria / Durham** - Another North East gem, this area has high-class gin joints and traditional pubs to suit all student tastes.
- **Edinburgh** - Drop in for a dram or two, or sample Scottish ale in any one of the top pubs in the Scottish capital.
- **Birmingham** - England's "second city" and an obvious choice. Broad Street is a must.
- **Nottingham** - East Midlands city

boasts everything from gastro pubs to quirky cocktail bars.

University places where options for solid boozing are aplenty.

- **Lancaster** - Cosy city, lots of pubs. Boozing potential? High.
- **Warwick** - Surprisingly large amount of pubs for a relatively small town. High concentration of thirsty students.
- **London** - One of only two "Alpha++" cities in the world (the other is New York), London doesn't need any introductions. Only value for money means it misses out on the Gold Award. Choice of boozers is among the best in the world.
- **Brighton / Sussex** - Tourism hotspot - thrives in the warmer months.

- **Exeter** - Large student base means Exeter is Devon's best boozing option.
- **Belfast** - Old and new merge to create a unique drinking environment built on a long-standing reputation.
- **Loughborough** - Highly-regarded university, notable for sport…and drinking.
- **Glasgow** - The urban sprawl of Scotland's largest city deserves a silver medal purely for its range of drinking opportunities.
- **Sheffield** - Thousands of students take advantage of South Yorkshire's plethora of bars and pubs.
- **Aberystwyth** - Previously mentioned as a Welsh hotspot for student tipples. Location of the National Library of Wales - a distraction for boozers.
- **Dundee** - Compact and easy to navigate, Dundee has seen a rise in pubs in recent years. Hardcore boozers welcome.

Not famous for boozing, but favourable nevertheless.

- **"Oxbridge"** - Internationally renowned, Oxford and Cambridge places learning above boozing, though there are several watering holes to keep a student's thirst at bay.
- **Edge Hill, Lancashire** - Close transport links with Liverpool means this Ormskirk university has loads of boozing opportunities.
- **St. Andrews** - Good range of boozers and bars to keep the town's thriving student population happy.
- **Reading** - A large town with excellent transport links to London will always appeal to the discerning boozer.
- **Bath** - Classic boozers mixed with

trendy bars, this historic city is brimming with opportunities for the thirsty student.

- **University of East Anglia (UEA... not to be confused with UAE)** - A bustling Student's Union in a city with more pubs than you can count (well, definitely on two hands).

- **Swansea** - Wales's "second city" is awash with both hard-hitting locals (pubs, not people) and student-friendly bars.

- **Hull** - Officially Kingston upon Hull, students head for the Old Town to drink in all it has to offer.

- **Plymouth** - One of the best drinking spots on the UK coast.

- **Honourable mentions:** Bournemouth, Surrey, Kent, Leicester.

Chapter 18: Trends, and drinking in culture

Boozing has undergone natural evolutions and trends, some of which can be seen to this day. When cheap wine, Taboo, 20/20, Hooch and snakebites were all the rage in the 1990s, nowadays there are microbreweries, American ales, "real" ales (see Chapter 5), flavoured ciders, wine clubs, rum menus and lavish gin joints. This isn't a bad thing - just an observation.

Global sales and marketing strategies will never disappear. Manufacturers and distributors know the importance of branding, so one thing that is certain: competition will remain fierce, and trends will continue to peak and trough in some sort of boozy evolution.

So which trends will surface in a few years? It's impossible to say. COVID has affected almost everything to some degree, with brand styles and trends altering to reflect the pandemic. What will emerge? Who knows? What is probably true is that there'll be something *new at some time in the near future.* Maybe more sustainable tipples? A growth in hard seltzers? A Pernod surge? Rhubarb Guinness? Wait and see…

One development in both the industry and consumer's preferences is the growing availability of low calorie beer. The reasons are varied, and should all be noted by any contemporary student. Consider the following:

- A low calorie tipple contains fewer carbohydrates - and less sugar.
- Greater all-round health awareness means that lower calorie drinks are *relevant.*
- There is now less stigma associated with

low calorie drinks.

- COVID times have changed some consumers' habits / opinions.
- Students like a drink - that much has been discussed. But it's already been highlighted that students shouldn't feel pressured into anything they're not comfortable with. Enjoying a low calorie beverage can be part of every student's drinking habit.

Luckily, there is a brand that is sure to be a hit with students everywhere. Skinny Lager by SkinnyBrands is a malty premium lager that has a refreshingly low 89 calories per bottle - equating to roughly 35% fewer calories than other premium lagers. Skinny Lager also contains 72% fewer carbs than other lagers, and is kosher, gluten free, vegan, as well as being 0.4% sugar. Students can now knock back a few bottles of "Skinnies" without the guilt sometimes associated with higher calorific brands. Happy days!

TOP LOW CALORIE LAGER BRAND

- ABV: 4%
- Taste: 10
- Value for Money: 10
- Innovation: 10
- Overall Student Rating: 10

Head to www.skinnybrands.com to discover the wonderful low calorie world of Skinny Lager!

*****

Another growth seen particularly in the beer

sector is the use of more natural ingredients in the brewing process. Beer is normally wonderfully simple in its composition, but if boosting the texture and flavour with, say, honey, improves the experience, then it's all good.

The best beer of its type is Hiver - a London brew that uses honey from independent beekeepers to produce crisp, light beers with subtle aromas. Award-winning, flavoursome and helping the urban and rural beekeeping communities all in one go, Hiver is a fine example of a beer trend that's been heading in the right direction since 2013.

*****

Business is business, but it helps if the brand

is both approachable and has an eye on modern trends. One of the best drinks brands in the country is North Brewing Co. Based in Yorkshire, this marvellous company operated the first craft beer bar in Britain, and now has other locations, a subscription service, customer vouchers and merchandise, along with numerous awards, including "Best Branding and Design" The Beer and Cider Marketing Awards 2018.

Notable drinking novels / memoirs

- *Hard Up Down Under* - Joe Varley. Young Brit drinks and works his way around New Zealand in boy-to-adult travel comedy.

- *The Lost Weekend* - Charles Jackson. Mid 1930s alcohol binge in Manhattan.
- *The Rum Diary* / *Fear and Loathing in Las Vegas* - Hunter S. Thompson. Gonzo goings-on from legendary on-the-edge journalist. (See films below).
- *Post Office* / *Factotum* - Charles Bukowski (See below). Autobiographical lowlife shenanigans by professional drinker.
- *Chump Change* / *Mooch* - Dan Fante. Ferocious booze blackouts by alter ego Bruno Dante.
- *Down By The River Where The Dead Men Go* - George Pelecanos. Washington D.C. private investigator Nick Stefanos undercovers sleazy crime amidst beer and shots of Old Grand-dad whiskey.
- *A Million Little Pieces* - James Frey. Controversial work penned as a "memoir", detailing addiction.
- *Leaving Las Vegas* - John O'Brien. Semi-autobiographical work, made into notable film about an alcoholic who drinks himself to death. (See films

below).

- *Wishful Drinking* - Carrie Fisher. Actress tells all involving a fair bit of boozing.
- *A Drop Of The Hard Stuff* - Lawrence Block. Crime novel featuring Matthew Scudder facing his demons.
- *On The Road* - Jack Kerouac. Hitchhiking across America, consuming booze and drugs. A 1950s classic.
- *Lit* - Mary Karr. Undeniably personal and boozy.
- *Dry* - Augusten Burroughs. Regular Joe boozes his way to rehab.

Plus…references to booze can be found in most books written by Ernest Hemingway (of course), Charles Dickens, F Scott Fitzgerald, James Crumley, Raymond Chandler, the works of William Shakespeare, James Ellroy, and in all matter of historical works.

…and films

- *Barfly* - Comedy drama based on Charles Bukowski's boozy (low)life. The legendary sloshed author even makes an appearance.

- *Withnail & I* - A student favourite. Two out-of-work pissheads go on holiday to Penrith by mistake. "We want the finest wines available to humanity! We want them here, and we want them now!" Class.

- *Leaving Las Vegas* - Alcoholic goes to "Sin City" to drink himself to death. Both tragic and funny, with Oscar-winning performances.

- *Swingers* - "Vegas, baby!" A cult classic about break-ups, friendships and nights on the town with whisky, as long as it's "any Glen".

- *Beerfest* - US comedy about two brothers travelling to Germany, only to realise a secret. Cue hilarity dubbed "Fight Club with beers". A lot of beer.

- *Drinking Buddies* - Soppy flick about friends and a brewery.

- *Flight* - Pilot saves passengers on his plane, but how? He was pissed.

- *Fear & Loathing in Las Vegas* - Journalist

reports in the city, taking too many drugs and consuming booze. What is it about Vegas?

- *Smashed* - Alkies wanting to become sober.
- *Crazy Heart* - Broken down country singer hits all the right notes by boozing.
- *The World's End* - Alien invasions during a pub crawl.
- *28 Days* - Predictable US offering focusing on rehab.
- *The Hangover* - Memory loss in Las Vegas on a bachelor's night out.
- *National Lampoon's Animal House* - Frat film starring the legendary John Belushi.
- *Superbad* - Successful US film regarding fake I.Ds and illicit booze.

...and best drinking songs?

Whether the theme is drinking itself, or simply a great tune to accompany boozing, these songs should appeal to most student drinkers.

- "Cryin' into the Beer of a Drunk Man"

- The New Bomb Turks. One of the best titles in punk.
- "Nightrain" - Guns N' Roses. Reference to notorious brand of fortified wine.
- "Tequila" - The Champs. 1950s hip-shaker, best played with shots.
- "Groove Is In The Heart" - Dee-Lite. One of the best party tunes; goes well with cocktails.
- "It's Five O'Clock Somewhere" - Alan Jackson and Jimmy Buffett. "I've been to Margaritaville a few times. All right, that's good. Stumbled all the way back…"
- "Tubthumping" - Chumbawamba. Played incessantly in the 90s. Four different drinks referred to in the lyrics.
- "Red Red Wine" - Neil Diamond / UB40. Alcohol is the only way to forget one's woes. "I'd have sworn that with time, thoughts of you leave my head. I was wrong, now I find just one thing makes me forget…"
- "Milk and alcohol" - Dr. Feelgood.

Perfect for the lactose-friendly booze-loving student.

- "(You Gotta) Fight for Your Right (To Party!)" - Beastie Boys. No explanation required.
- Anything by Motörhead.
- "I Gotta Get Drunk" - Willie Nelson. And he sure does dread it…
- "I'm Always Drunk in San Francisco (And I Don't Drink At All)" - Nancy Wilson. One for the city's tourist board?
- "One Scotch, One Bourbon, One Beer" - Amos Milburn. "Please mister bartender, listen here, I ain't here for trouble, so have no fear."
- "The 900 Number" - The 45 King. Put it on a 10 minute loop and get up to get down.

Facts and stats to dazzle every drinker

Be a pub legend by relaying some of these boozy facts:

- The "Nastro Azzurro" of Peroni

translates as "blue ribbon" - the lager's logo (although most Italians prefer the red stuff).

- James Bond's "Vesper" cocktail is three measures of Gordon's gin, one of vodka, half a measure of Kina Lillet, shaken well until it's ice cold, served with with a large thin slice of lemon peel. Even the coolest man finds solace in alcohol.

- The stately woman on the logo of Bombay Sapphire gin is none other than Queen Victoria.

- It is reported that there are approximately 49 million bubbles in a standard bottle of Champagne.

- The five points of Newcastle Brown Ale's iconic blue star logo represent Newcastle's five founding breweries.

- The name of the Spanish lager Estrella Damm is derived from the Spanish for "star" (its logo) and the name of the brewer of the original recipe - August Kuentzmann Damm.

- The first press advert for Guinness was

in 1929. The slogan "Guinness is Good for You" is one of the most recognised slogans of all time.

- Bacardi's logo is a bat. This arose from the founder's wife, Dona Amalia, who noticed a fruit bat colony hanging from the rafters of the original distillery - the flying animals were a symbol of health, good fortune and family unity.
- The oldest known winery is Armenian.
- There are blue wines, which are a combination of red and white grapes with the dye indigotine.
- "Claret" wines are from Bordeaux.
- Alabama is the only US state to have an alcoholic state drink: whiskey. Milk is most other state's official drink.
- The founder of Jameson Irish Whiskey, John Jameson, was Scottish.
- A "magnum" wine bottle is equivalent to two standard wine bottles - i.e. 1.5 litres. The word is Latin for "great".
- 2019's World Bartender of the Year was Andris Reizenbergs from Latvia.

- The International Bartenders Association has three main categories for cocktails: "The Unforgettables" (e.g. Manhattan), "Contemporary Classics" (e.g. Cosmopolitan) and "New Era Drinks" (e.g. Suffering Bastard - look it up!)
- The man behind Crystal Head vodka is acting legend Dan Aykroyd (check out his drunken scene dressed up as Santa Claus in *Trading Places* for top boozing acting).
- Oktoberfest in Munich is the world's largest beer festival. Most of it takes place in September. According to *Guinness World Records,* in 2013 the festival attracted 6.9 million people, with 7.5 million litres of beer consumed on a site as big as 1,600 tennis courts.
- The world record for most cocktails made in an hour by one person is an astonishing 1,905.
- Pimm's is a brand of "fruit cup". The most famous is No.1, and is gin-based.

The recipe for the Original Pimm's No.1 is: Highball glass filled with ice, 50ml Pimm's No.1, 150ml lemonade, add strawberry & orange & cucumber, sprig of mint. N.B. Pimm's No.6 contains vodka.

- The country with the highest beer consumption per capita is Czech Republic (Czechia). In 2011, nearly 145 litres were bought per head.

Chapter 19: Safety first and wellbeing

Student life is a liberty associated with all sorts of new experiences. Whilst being street smart is helpful in all aspects of adult life, living away from home at university often opens more diverse doors for a lot of students. Even if your university location allows frequent home visits, student life can be challenging. Whatever your situation, help is always available.

We've established that drinking can (and should) be fun, but should also be treated with respect. Students should never underestimate the potential dangers. If you're concerned about your (or someone else's drinking), Drink Aware is a recommended independent charity that offers all kinds of help, facts and guidance on drinking. Visit www.drinkaware.co.uk.

Of course, there are plenty of other helpful options. Friends, Student Unions, GPs, tutors…a student has a plethora of helping hands to be used when necessary. The worst

Joe varley

thing to do is to remain silent.

Mental health is a subject that has received more exposure recently, and therefore is now less of a social stigma. It can be a complicated - and tricky - subject to broach. As with drinking issues, help is readily available, so don't suffer in silence. CALM (Campaign Against Living Miserably) - a leading movement against suicide - is a notable website to view for help and support. Check them out at www.thecalmzone.net. Alternatively, go to www.mind.org.uk

Student Unions offer valuable advice on the following issues:

- Bullying / social media abuse.
- Crime.
- Welfare and community.
- Women's concerns.
- Racism.
- Housing / hardship funds.
- LGBTQ (Lesbian, Gay, Bisexual, Transgender, Questioning / Queer).
- Zero tolerance / sexual harassment /

violence.

- Students living with disabilities.
- However lonely or ostracised a student may feel, talking and getting the right help at the right moment is vital.

Chapter 20: Student survival guide checklist

Hopefully you, dear reader, will have learnt something from this book.

The general guidance is to have fun, but to *respect booze*. "A wasted weekend is never a weekend wasted"…or is it "a weekend wasted is never a wasted weekend"? It doesn't matter; either way you had fun.

Whatever you absorb from this book (apart from beer stains), stick to these 12 points and you won't go far wrong at university:

- ✓ Experiment with alcohol, but…
- ✓ …be sensible.
- ✓ Enjoy.
- ✓ Respect other people's preferences.
- ✓ Be street smart / safe.
- ✓ Don't let anyone tell you that boozing is wrong. It's not, if done correctly and responsibly.

- ✓ Embrace the whole university experience.

- ✓ Try online options - there are great drinks options for students other than pubs or supermarkets.

- ✓ Watch your finances.

- ✓ Treat drinking games with caution.

- ✓ Respect bar staff and comply with the long arm of the law.

- ✓ Make as many friends as possible.

Which leaves a departing comment:

Good luck with student / college life. Study hard, socialise, make lots of friends, and consider the time at university the best of your life.

Whether you graduate with a "First", a "Two-One", a "Desmond" ("Two-Two"), a "Third" or a "Pass", you should be genuinely invigorated and have aspirations of conquering the "real world".

And even if you leave university with the degree you hadn't hoped for, at least you'll have a "FiB" - "First in Boozing".

Cheers!

Cut-out and keep "pub rating" cards - useful *and* stylish!

Name of boozer:

Price rating:

Student friendly rating:

Booze rating:

Worth a revisit? Yes   No

Name of boozer:

Price rating:

Student friendly rating:

Booze rating:

Worth a revisit? Yes   No

Joe varley

Lightning Source UK Ltd.
Milton Keynes UK
UKHW021132241121
394474UK00005B/311

9 781914 560095